CIRCUIT TRAIN YOUR BRAIN
Daily Habits That Develop Resilience

Molly M. Cantrell-Kraig

BALBOA
PRESS
A DIVISION OF HAY HOUSE

Copyright © 2019 Molly M. Cantrell-Kraig.

All rights reserved. No part of this book may be used or reproduced by any means, graphic, electronic, or mechanical, including photocopying, recording, taping or by any information storage retrieval system without the written permission of the author except in the case of brief quotations embodied in critical articles and reviews.

This book is a work of non-fiction. Unless otherwise noted, the author and the publisher make no explicit guarantees as to the accuracy of the information contained in this book and in some cases, names of people and places have been altered to protect their privacy.

Balboa Press books may be ordered through booksellers or by contacting:

Balboa Press
A Division of Hay House
1663 Liberty Drive
Bloomington, IN 47403
www.balboapress.com
1 (877) 407-4847

Because of the dynamic nature of the Internet, any web addresses or links contained in this book may have changed since publication and may no longer be valid. The views expressed in this work are solely those of the author and do not necessarily reflect the views of the publisher, and the publisher hereby disclaims any responsibility for them.

The author of this book does not dispense medical advice or prescribe the use of any technique as a form of treatment for physical, emotional, or medical problems without the advice of a physician, either directly or indirectly. The intent of the author is only to offer information of a general nature to help you in your quest for emotional and spiritual well-being. In the event you use any of the information in this book for yourself, which is your constitutional right, the author and the publisher assume no responsibility for your actions.

Any people depicted in stock imagery provided by Getty Images are models, and such images are being used for illustrative purposes only. Certain stock imagery © Getty Images.

Print information available on the last page.

ISBN: 978-1-9822-2364-9 (sc)
ISBN: 978-1-9822-2366-3 (hc)
ISBN: 978-1-9822-2365-6 (e)

Library of Congress Control Number: 2019903057

Balboa Press rev. date: 03/27/2019

Dedication

To my daughters,
Phoenix, Mackenzie & Elizabeth
my first stakeholders

Contents

Chapter 1	Just Breathe	1
Chapter 2	Wash it Away	3
Chapter 3	Wake Up and Smell the Coffee!	5
Chapter 4	The Answer is Blowing in the Wind	7
Chapter 5	Check it Out	9
Chapter 6	Small Stuff Makes a Big Difference	10
Chapter 7	Attitude of Gratitude	13
Chapter 8	Yuk it Up, Fuzzball	17
Chapter 9	Crank Up the Jams	20
Chapter 10	Get Down and Dirty	22
Chapter 11	Hero Worship	25
Chapter 12	It's a Dog's Life	26
Chapter 13	The Metaphysics of Chocolate	28
Chapter 14	Good Morning, Starshine	30
Chapter 15	Take a Note	32
Chapter 16	Tug o'war vs. Hug o'war	34
Chapter 17	How to Find Your Purpose	35
Chapter 18	Get Bent	39
Chapter 19	Mind Your Manners	42
Chapter 20	Splish Splash	44
Chapter 21	"I get by with a little help from my friends." – The Beatles	46
Chapter 22	Bust a Move	49

Chapter 23	Paradox is a Hoot	50
Chapter 24	Take a Grass Bath	52
Chapter 25	Pay It Forward	53
Chapter 26	Nothing Ventured; Nothing Gained	55
Chapter 27	Oil Be There for You	61
Chapter 28	Channel Your Inner George Bailey	64
Chapter 29	Orange You Glad ?	68
Chapter 30	Daydream Believer – Channeling Your Woo Woo Katchoo	71
Chapter 31	Grandma's Ghost	75
Chapter 32	Hearing vs. Listening	77
Chapter 33	Fire It Up	80
Chapter 34	Dorothy Parker Was Right	82
Chapter 35	Here There Be Dragons	86
Chapter 36	How to Recognize Miracles	91
Chapter 37	More, Please	94

Acknowledgments

I've made reference to having an Inner Sanctum in previous writings. These are the people in my orbit who have received texts from me at weird hours of the day, some of which simply say, "I'm not crazy, and this will all work out." Their consistent and patient reply was always, "You're not crazy, and this will all work out."

There have been a few times in my life when things have gone south, and rather than desert me, these individuals are those who have drawn closer to make sure I don't stumble. In the face of financial collapse, betrayal, personal or professional challenges, I have been blessed to know kind, loving and intelligent people who have helped me gather the pieces of my broken life and help me mend it.

Resilience is built one brick at a time, through loving actions. Like all good networks and supports, these bricks are forged and laid way before they are needed. I think they are the supports Ray Bradbury alluded to in his quote about leaping off a cliff and building your wings on the way down.

In listing acknowledgements, my biggest fear is that I will forget someone. With that being said, in no particular order, I would like to thank Amy Oscar, Dave Howard, Staci Jordan Shelton, Ronald O'Neal, Jr., Hope Bertram, Connie Burke, Ric Dragon,

Liz Strauss, Chris Gair, Jane Boyd, Jim Feeney, Desiree Adaway, Bradley H. Smith, Nicole Yeary, Adam Shake, Marcy Capron Vermillion, David Brown, Lisa Petrilli, Angel Djambazov, Melissa Pierce, Jeremy Fischbach, Amy Guth, David S. Silverman, Mana Ionescu, Marti Konstant and Shashi Bellamkonda.

Without their presence in my life, this book would not exist.

And above all, I would like to acknowledge the impact of my daughters for fashioning me into the woman I am today. They give me a reason to wake up every day and try again.

Best,
M.

Prologue

There had to be a dime somewhere.

It was almost midnight, and my eyes swept cracks in the floor at the 24-hour grocers, searching for loose change. Food stamps wouldn't pay for the non-food items like the laundry detergent in my cart, and I was a few cents short. Seeing no coins, I realized that I would have to do without the soap.

Resignedly, I put the box back on the shelf and died just a little bit inside, knowing that I didn't have the cash to buy it. I was shopping in the wee hours of the morning as my daughter slept in her crib at my mother's farmhouse a few miles away.

Using food stamps was always a struggle for me, because of the shame I felt. Enduring the judgment of others only made it worse, so I did my shopping when I had less chance of encountering others.

Deep in my heart, I knew that I was in the wrong place – my intelligence and ambition should have vaulted me elsewhere. But here I was, scrounging for change to purchase soap in a grocery store in the dead of night.

How did I get here? How was I going to change my life? Where should I begin?

When I thought about it a bit more, I asked myself, what did it matter? I felt like a failure.

This was a low point in my life twenty-some years ago, and at the time, I didn't see any light at the end of the tunnel. My immediate future was bleak. I was living with my mom, eking out an existence on public aid and having little to no direction beyond the immediate.

How did I get here?

I arrived on this planet broken. Literally. My heart was malformed due to a congenital heart defect. Congenital means 'present at birth,' and doesn't refer to a genetic condition. I wasn't expected to live, and it was only through a radical surgery called Tetralogy of Fallot that my heart condition was corrected.

While I wasn't a sickly child (I was raised with a 'shake it off' mentality), I did spend a lot of time in hospitals when I was young. As a result, I learned to read when I was three years old and was precocious. Add to this being an eldest child, and you have the makings for someone with the predisposition for being driven and upon whom high expectations were placed. To be fair, I have always, always been my harshest critic. I think we all are our worst critics.

But I was also someone who grew up without a true north. I wasn't exactly sure how to harness and channel my intrinsic compulsion to achieve. Add to this my having an inborn curiosity without the ability to focus and the result is a ball of energy with no outlet. It was extremely frustrating for me.

Unlike some, however, I was lucky enough to have an art teacher who was able to channel some of my creative talents and helped me to transition them to a larger world. As an art student in high school, I was the only one who was given permission to create my own curriculum. For two years, I was graded not only on my ability to craft and assign my own projects, but I was also able to explore multiple expressions of what art meant for me.

When I was a junior in high school, I began receiving recruitment materials from the Parson's School of Design in Los Angeles and New York. How exciting! It fed an exceptionalism and focus for me in a way I had never considered. In addition, my art teacher had submitted my work to a prestigious midwestern college for inclusion in a juried regional exhibition.

I can still remember arriving in the huge city where the college was located and walking into a room full of artsy types, clad head-to-toe in black (which happened to be my de facto preferred look). Two opposing impressions still linger in my mind:

1. Good: Having grown up in a very small town in Iowa, it was encouraging to see other people like me. They dressed like me. Their handwriting (ALL CAPS) was like mine. I felt as though I was among my own people.
2. Bad: There were some students whose work was leagues ahead of my own. Their talent was breathtaking (and intimidating). I felt an immediate gut punch and the stirrings of Imposter Syndrome churning in my stomach. Who was I to be among these people? Perhaps my teacher had made a mistake.

Gathering my courage, I presented my portfolio to the first jurist sitting behind the massive tables. He opened my book and flicked through its pages before pausing. He then peered over his glasses, glanced at me over the top of the rims and closed my portfolio.

"I have never seen anything more puerile," he said. "There is no sophistication or anything of interest in your work."

Even as I type these sentences, my heart is fluttering like a trip-hammer in my throat, my fingers are trembling, and tears threaten to spill from my eyes. Stupefied, I collected my portfolio from him and, with shaky legs, proceeded down the tables to the next jurists.

It wasn't until I had shown my work to four more people that I finally heard the words of one gentleman breaking through through my stupor. He looked at my sketches and said, "This one here shows depth and sensitive expression." He kept talking, but I really didn't hear him. My blood was rushing to my head; my knees were knocking, and the imposter voice was screaming in my head, saying, "YOU ARE A FRAUD AND HAVE BEEN RECOGNIZED FOR THE TALENTLESS, SMALL-TOWN NOBODY THAT YOU REALLY ARE."

As soon as I left the room, I vomited in the nearest bathroom.

From an adult's perspective, I now recognize the first jurist as perhaps a frustrated artist himself, whose only joy may have been gained through criticizing others. Maybe he had fought with his partner that morning and was still in a fit of pique. Who knows? What I do know is that I have come to recognize and respect the awesome power of words and the pain they can inflict. Words also have the power to uplift, empower, inspire and energize.

Dejected, I went home and put my dreams in a box, preparing to hitch my wagon to someone else's star. After all, I was pretty and sweet. Someone would save me. I would reach my dreams through someone else.

In writing this book, I was forced to really examine my life choices and how they contributed to my journey and the person I am today. It may seem laughable, considering that I have a digital footprint in several social media platforms, but I'm actually a pretty private person.

However, in order to give this book real heft, establish my street cred and authenticity, it's crucial that you understand that the lessons I'll be sharing with you grew from stupendous failure and poor choices.

Saturday Night Live comic, the late Gilda Radner once said, "There is no real security except for whatever you build inside yourself."

I first read this quote in 1997. By this time, I had three young daughters and was working at a daily newspaper. I was a single mother, having recently been divorced.

For much of my life, I transferred ownership of my independence and security to others: boyfriends, spouses, bosses…anyone but the person upon whom the responsibility rested (me). Gilda's words galvanized me into action, henceforth accepting responsibility for my own choices. But I'm getting ahead of myself…

I married a man because he asked me to.

I was very young when I met him and was already mother to a toddler. I therefore felt as though I was "used goods." Believing no man would want me, when this man asked me to marry him, I thought that I had better say yes before he changed his mind. During the marriage ceremony, my soul gave one last ditch effort to pull me back from the brink, hurling the equivalent of a mental "Hail Mary Pass" across my brain, shrieking, "What are you doing?!"

My answer to myself, "Everything's paid for." (meaning the reception)

Everything is paid for. I'll say it was.

I paid, and I paid again. It took seven years of my life to pay myself the interest on that decision. During those seven years, I had to face myself, do an assessment of where I was developmentally against what I was capable of achieving, and then take steps each day toward reaching my goals. Along the way, I had teachers, employers, colleagues and friends helping me to develop skills and strengths, but ultimately, it was up to me to choose better for myself.

I know what it's like to be scared. I know what it's like to feel that gnawing sense that you're missing the mark – that you're meant for greater things. And I also know the emancipating thrill of knowing that you're where you're meant to be.

You cannot borrow security. You must invest in yourself. It is through this investment that you develop resilience. Each failure creates an opportunity for 'bouncing back,' thus strengthening your soul's elasticity.

Maybe you're in the same spot right now. Maybe you're feeling like an imposter. Maybe you've made some poor choices. Maybe you're going through a really rough patch and don't see a way out. Maybe you're being bullied. Maybe you live in a dysfunctional home where abuse is present.

Do you feel as if your life is on an endless loop – a downward spiral from which there is no escape? Consider this: you are where you are supposed to be. Paradoxically, it is when you've reached the point of giving up, that you are poised to begin something entirely new. To paraphrase author J.K. Rowling, your rock bottom is the foundation upon which you can build your future. You matter.

But how do you flip the switch? How do you develop resilience? How can you bounce back from misfortune?

All change begins within before it shows up in your life. Your thoughts are powerful levers that shift your perspective, which in turn changes your life. But what if you were raised in a family of pessimists? What if you aren't used to thinking in terms of the best possible scenario? What if you've been trained to think that optimists are suckers – fools who don't understand "the way things really are?"

In an extremely oversimplified answer, your brain is a computer of sorts. By changing your thought patterns, you may essentially reprogram the way you think. Once your brain accepts its new settings, you may see opportunities where you once saw none. You will naturally gravitate toward possibility. You will be in a better position to recognize and allow abundance into your life.

It all starts by doing something different each day.

For me, at some point, I leveraged the accumulated lessons I learned as a single mother to establish a nonprofit organization designed to help other single mothers emancipate themselves economically. The organization was recognized by the Huffington Post in 2013, so once my youngest daughter was ready to head off to college, I chose to move to Chicago to expand its scale and scope.

To prepare for the transition, before I moved to the Windy City at age forty-five to expand this nonprofit, I held what I refer to as "The Living Funeral." I had to remove what no longer served me to make space for my new life to emerge.

To begin, I stacked a pile of stuff that I wanted to keep in the move to Chicago in my bedroom: my bed, my books, and a few sentimental items. The rest of my worldly possessions were organized in my living and dining rooms, where I invited family and close friends to essentially pick through my belongings, taking what they wanted.

When they had chosen the items they wished to have, the rest of the heap was placed on my front lawn for a yard sale. Further winnowed down, what remained after the sale got boxed up and went straight to the thrift store donation bin.

The rest was loaded onto a U-Haul, and I was on my way.

Thusly liberated, I started over with essentially nothing in a city of over three million souls. It was a pretty big leap. As a point of reference, in a city of seventy-seven neighborhoods, the neighborhood where I live has three times as many people in it as the mid-sized city I left in Iowa.

My move to Chicago began a six-year transition period full of additional learning opportunities. Adjusting to a huge metropolitan area presented many challenges, especially for a small town girl who was in way over her head. Change at this scale wrought unpleasant side effects and required great sacrifice. There were many nights that I slept in a parka with a heating pad at my feet because I didn't have the income to keep the furnace at a comfortable level.

I woke up scared. A lot. I took Epsom salt baths and burned away panic-penned letters in the dead of night. I faced eviction not once, but twice, within five years.

More than once, I made decisions based on the sequence of "fire, aim, ready," or leaping before looking. Those are stories for another time, but everything that you'll read in this book was used by me at some point to reorient my brain, build resilience and to program it for a perspective of gratitude and abundance rather than scarcity.

This book is intended to introduce daily habits designed to change up the wiring in your head. Each day contains a new thought, experience or exercise that will help shift your perspective and the patterns in your thinking.

Full disclosure: not all of these suggestions will resonate with everyone. Some days, the prompt will not seem to apply to you or your situation. However, I promise that if you faithfully show up for yourself every day and use this book as it is intended, your life will change for the better. You will be a changed person – stronger and ready to step into the highest version of yourself.

Ready to begin? Let's go.

***

How to use this book

> Get comfortable with being alone.
>
>> "I am Me. Because I own all of me, I can become intimately acquainted with me. By so doing, I can love me and be friendly with all my parts. I know there are aspects about myself that puzzle me, and other aspects that I do not know – but as long as I am friendly and loving to myself, I can courageously and hopefully look for solutions to the puzzles and ways to find out more about me. I own me, and therefore, I can engineer me. I am me, and I am Okay." - Virginia Satir, American psychotherapist and educator

Resilience is fostered through internally-driven or choices made about and for oneself. Whether living with fear or faith or how to harness one's fear, being comfortable with being alone is essential to living out the consequences of our choices.

Many people make their decisions based upon their ability to be alone – for both personal and professional reasons. Some people remain in unfulfilling relationships or soul-sucking jobs because they do not want to be alone. For some, the devil they know is better than the devil they don't; they view being alone in a negative light.

Are you able to be alone?

Comfort with being alone is more than just being okay with doing a stint in solitary confinement. Being alone requires an ability to accept and acknowledge who you are (both the good and bad parts) independent of anyone else. It requires an ability to trust yourself. Resilience means, in some respects, to be able to rely on yourself.

Without the ability to accept, trust and love oneself, no true foundation can be built for your life.

Buy a separate notebook for the exercises we'll be using. While you won't use this notebook every day, it must have a design that makes you smile when you see it. Reaching for this notebook is something that you want to look forward to doing, rather than viewing it as a chore. Use a pen or pencil that feels good in your hand.

Here are a few tools we'll use throughout this book to help cultivate an awareness of yourself:

Journaling: Rather than a literal list of the day's events, use journal entries to ask yourself questions like these:

> What did I learn today?
> What about today made me the happiest?
> Where did I spend my energy?
> What would I like to accomplish?

Meditation: Just by spending 15 minutes in silence and concentrating on your breathing, you can gain a greater awareness of yourself. It's very difficult to quiet your mind, but not impossible. As thoughts flit across your consciousness, acknowledge and release them. Eventually, with enough practice, you'll gain greater control over your mind.

Yoga: Even something as basic as stretching for a small amount of time each day can help you become more aware of your physical self. Yoga helps to heighten your senses, your flexibility and fitness.

Look back at times in your life where you were alone. What were the positive aspects of these periods? What made you uncomfortable?

Commit to reading a chapter from the book first thing in the morning. No excuses. First thing. Some of the chapters are longer than others. The exercises are designed to take less than twenty minutes.

You are worth twenty minutes.

Take the time. Make the time. The mere act of showing up for yourself each day will begin to shift the world in your favor. I promise.

As you spend time with yourself, sift out the parts you would like to develop while recognizing the things that you like about yourself. Understanding what makes us special helps us contribute to the quality of life for not only ourselves but our families, friends and communities. NOTE: do not focus on what's missing as you sift. Focus on what is going well. Focus on what is present. By focusing on what is going well, you will create a channel for more to flow toward you. When you focus on what's missing or what you are doing "wrong," you will reinforce lack, or scarcity.

Self care is not selfish.

By paying attention to our own voices, we can discern what we value as opposed to what society tells us we should value. Having information like this helps us to chose situations that will foster resilience and build independence, including financial, personal and professional. Having that point of reference and certainty in ourselves ultimately makes us more effective people.

A new habit that I highly recommend cultivating is to say each and every day to yourself, "I am worthy of good things." To make sure that you have a chance to foster this habit, I have included it at the end of each chapter. I encourage you to say it aloud each time you see it.

Chapter One
Just Breathe

In addition to being the title of my favorite Pearl Jam song, breath forms the beginning of your new life. One of my most oft-used phrases is, "oxygen cures everything." Breathing is the source of your power, your focus and your life. It is the animating force that fuels your cells and your brain.

How many times throughout the day are you aware of your breathing? Most of the time, we breathe shallowly, barely plumbing the depths of our lungs' capacity. We're going to start this book with an intentional, mindful focus on how you breathe.

Breathe in through your nose. Expand your lungs fully, until you can feel your rib cage stretch. Now exhale, pretending that you are blowing out a candle across the room. Make sure that your stomach completely deflates as you exhale. Blow until your stomach is "empty." Inhale deeply again, expanding your rib cage. If it helps, lie down with your back against the floor as you breathe. Gravity will force your body to breathe properly. Repeat this process five times.

This breathing exercise begins the process of clearing out negative energy.

Every time you feel yourself tense up today, repeat this exercise until it becomes second nature. Again, oxygen cures everything. By making sure that your brain and your cells are properly oxygenated, you are providing them with the raw materials to operate at their highest level.

- Inhale. ...Exhale.
- Inhale. ...Exhale.
- Inhale. ...Exhale.
- Inhale. ...Exhale.
- Inhale. ...Exhale.

For some help on the timing and cadence of how to breathe, you may wish to do a Google search for "breathing gif," and a number of visual examples will populate the results. Use these to pace your breathing until it becomes second nature.

Say aloud to yourself, "I am worthy of good things."

Chapter Two
Wash it Away

You were probably thirsty when you woke up this morning. Your body performs a lot of maintenance while you sleep, and that kind of work creates waste that needs to be carried out of your body.

About sixty percent of the average adult human body is made of water, according to a National Institutes of Health report. This includes most of your brain, heart, lungs, muscles and skin, and even about thirty percent of your bones. Besides being one of the main ingredients in the recipe for your body, water helps us regulate our internal temperature, transports nutrients throughout our bodies, flushes waste, forms saliva, lubricates joints and even serves as a protective shock absorber for vital organs.

To keep your human, carbon-based machine running at top form, you must drink enough water. Today's exercise is to drink a full eight ounces of water before you eat breakfast or make your coffee. As you swallow, imagine the water flowing through your veins, clearing away the collected debris from the night's restoration of your body.

For extra credit: consider getting a bottle that holds thirty-two ounces of water and commit to drinking one of these bottles full of water each day. To help jog your memory, there are hydration apps for your smartphone that can remind you when to drink water, or you can create calendar alerts yourself. Whatever works.

By properly hydrating your body, you are helping to operate at your highest level. Your brain will be sharper; your metabolism will elevate, and your skin will glow.

Say aloud to yourself, "I am worthy of good things."

Chapter Three
Wake Up and Smell the Coffee!

If you haven't caught on by now, these first few chapters represent baby steps toward the new you by bringing things back to basics: our senses and our mechanics of operation. If your body isn't firing on all cylinders, nothing you do will fundamentally change the way things are happening for you in your life.

As an analogy as it relates to resilience: a flat basketball will not bounce. A full one will. Your body must be "full" in order for it to bounce back from the challenges life will throw at you.

Lasting change happens on a subconscious level before it can fully manifest on the surface level. The triumvirate of body – mind – spirit must work in balance in order to create your best results and strongest self.

Today, we'll focus on the senses of smell and touch.

Begin by brewing a fresh cup of coffee (or tea). Really pay attention to the steps as you do this.

Give thanks for the water that pours from the tap. You didn't have to walk five miles to draw it from a well. You didn't have to pick any leaves out of it, nor jostle for shoulder space next to a water buffalo in order to access it. It streamed like magic from your tap at the flick of your wrist.

Before you scoop the coffee into the filter, stick your nose into the container and smell the grounds. Feel the scent climb into your brain, waking up the cells inside it.

As your coffee perks (or tea steeps), touch your toes. Stretch. Feel your muscles flex. Say thank you.

Once you pour the fragrant elixir into your mug, feel the warmth from the coffee spread into your fingers. Inhale and take a sip. Once in a while, I will actually raise my mug to no one in particular and say, "cheers" while standing in my kitchen. True story.

Say aloud to yourself, "I am worthy of good things."

Chapter Four
The Answer is Blowing in the Wind

Step outside if weather permits. For the most part, unless your neighborhood is experiencing a natural disaster like a tornado or hurricane, weather will permit. Put on a coat if it's cold, but go outside.

Notice the way your body reacts to the weather. Feel the sun on your face. Consider the way your nose hairs freeze if it's a winter day. Inhale deeply through your nose.

What do you smell? Damp leaves? Petrichor? Freshly cut grass? Flowers?

Is there a rainstorm on the horizon? Consider the way the air shifts right before a storm. You can usually sense a change in the air pressure. Sometimes you can see a difference in the sky.

If you are going through a figurative storm in your life (job loss, death of a relationship or family member etc.), take heart: storms oftentimes blow through our lives in order to make space for what's coming.

When you step back inside, sit down and take a moment to jot down a few things in your notebook:

What are things you can release?

What no longer serves you?

What would you like to have more of in your life?

Simply by writing these down, you have activated the research centers that exist deep within your brain. Be alert for signs of their solutions as you go about your day.

Say aloud to yourself, "I am worthy of good things."

Chapter Five
Check it Out

When was the last time you visited a library? Today, I would like you to make plans to visit your nearest branch. If that's not possible, go to the library's website and learn about a program they offer or an event they're hosting that will expand your options and perception of the world.

Above and beyond being a repository for reading materials to lend, libraries are a source of classes, training, author events and other incredible opportunities to add to your base of knowledge.

Focusing on your notebook entry from yesterday, choose one of the three writing prompts and see how you can apply them to your visit to the library.

Perhaps there is a class on a subject you'd like to learn more about? Maybe the library is hosting an author whose life experience matches your goals? There may be a social group that meets at the library that discusses a habit you'd like to release?

Make a plan to follow up with a visit to your local library. Each book represents a brain, you know. Learning from the pages within add to your experiences and expands your opportunities.

Say aloud to yourself, "I am worthy of good things."

Chapter Six
Small Stuff Makes a Big Difference

When you're down in the dumps or faced with seemingly insurmountable odds, it helps to think small. It's easy to get overwhelmed, especially when your world looks like a tornado hit it. The damage can seem so big that we get paralyzed into inaction.

That said, barring an asteroid or meteor strike, the sun will come up tomorrow. With each new day, you have the chance at a new life.

While it's true that you can't turn the Queen Mary around on a dime, consider that she is steered by a comparatively small rudder. Same with your life. Your life is a 'big ship,' and making changes will take consistent, incremental effort to have a lasting effect. Physics is a thing, and your environment is no different. Big trajectories and changes may be created by your small actions, repeated daily.

That said, consider the number of factors, experiences and people who intersect with your life. Sometimes, your wait times will be influenced by the readiness and timetables of others. Get used to focusing on your efforts, and release the outcomes.

Mindfulness is probably one of the most difficult traits to cultivate. Many of us spend a lot of our time living in regret, nursing grudges or worrying about things that may or may not happen. It's so very ingrained in our individual and collective consciousnesses, that to jettison the past and the future takes a focused, concentrated effort. And it's an effort that must be lived each day, moment to moment.

What's frustrating about living in two time periods, like the past or the future (time periods that don't technically exist any more – or yet) is that in so doing, we lack the ability to truly harness the present. What's key to developing resilience is learning how to tap into the power of the present, because it is within the present that the true fulcrum of our efforts exists.

When we have the ability to notice, catalogue, discern and apply what is happening in the here and now, we have the best tools at our disposal for fashioning our future. If we're distracted by what has already happened, or worry about what has yet to come, we aren't paying attention to what's happening now. As a result, we're operating on less-than-complete intel.

Think right now of just one *teeny tiny* thing you could do that would change your life – whatever it is that immediately pops into your head, begin doing it today.

    Take a different route to work.

    Brush your teeth with your non-dominant hand.

Walk up a flight of stairs backwards.

Those small reversals or changes carve new synaptic channels into your brain. They shake things up, and when disruption happens at any level, opportunities reveal themselves.

Also: remember that great oaks don't arrive on this planet thirty-five feet tall and in full leaf. They grow from acorns. With this in mind:

    Nurture where you are

    Grow your network of "roots"

    Stay flexible

    Reach for the sky

Say aloud to yourself, "I am worthy of good things."

Chapter Seven
Attitude of Gratitude

There are many who encourage the practice of ending each day with listing things for which they are grateful. It's a good practice. But I have also found it to be true that beginning a day in the same fashion allows you to establish and frame the energy of the day from the outset.

For today's exercise, I'd like you to say 'thank you' for the next ten things that happen to you or that you encounter – good or bad. For additional energy toward this exercise, write them down in your handy-dandy notebook.

Some ideas include:

> Thank you for this day (I say this every morning before I get out of bed).
>
> Thank you for the ability to read.
>
> Thank you for the coffee (or tea) in my cup.
>
> Thank you for indoor plumbing.
>
> Thank you for a job or purpose today.

Thank you for my friend, _____ .

Thank you for the ability to hear/see/taste.

Thank you for the ability to make choices.

Thank you for the food in my pantry.

Thank you for a mind that can perceive.

How many of us can recall the last time we expressed gratitude? How many of us rejoiced this morning because their computer that connects them to the world started right up? ...That they can access cat videos from the confines of their snuggly bed while on their smartphone? That they'll probably be able to goof off today and watch sportsball with their friends – maybe even have a beer or two? That they can stand under a hot shower until someone flushes the toilet in the downstairs bath and yells at them to get the heck out of the bathroom?

These may all sound like goofy excuses for gratitude (especially that last one), but gratitude is not only the seat of all abundance, it is also key to activating your resilience. It is through rejoicing and gratitude that you identify that which is important to you. When you know what is important to you, you can divest yourself from the other stuff that the world says should be important to you. That, my friend, is some serious freedom.

So now I really take the time to notice when things are going well. I notice how good coffee smells when making the first pot of the day. ...watching the sun set and seeing the buttery-right-before-sunset glow reflect in the glassy silhouettes of the Chicago skyscrapers ...the sound of a kid laughing on the train. All of these are moments that are easily ignored, but they are all gifts waiting to be recognized.

By the way, this gratitude list goes for the "bad" things, too. For example, if you stub your toe on a table, say thank you for having a functioning neural net that allows your body to send, receive and interpret pain signals. If you step on an errant LEGO, give thanks for healthy children with architectural leanings.

Even when things aren't so Hallmark-ian, it pays to rejoice: when you lose the big account; when you lock yourself out of your car; when you date the wrong person. Each is a gift, waiting for you to see the lesson within so that you can apply it to tomorrow's actions.

The key is to begin to train your brain to see the good in all things.

Review your list, and if you can thank someone for an experience within the list, send them a quick email or a handwritten note, expressing your gratitude. For example:

> Dear First Grade Teacher,
>
> Thank you so much for instilling in me a love of reading. I'm sure it must have been overwhelming to teach such a wriggly audience, but having a teacher like you made a big difference. It's fun for me to take my own kids to the library today, where we take turns picking out our favorite books.
>
> I hope you're enjoying your retirement, and again, my thanks for the influence you had in my life.

Sincerely,

Grateful Student

Taking the extra step of "snail mailing" a thanks will turbocharge your exercise. I promise. An additional guarantee: If you repeat this chapter's exercise step at least three times a week, you will change your life exponentially.

The choices we make today do have an influence on our tomorrows. This is the fulcrum to which I alluded earlier. When we have the presence of mind to apply an awareness of what is happening now, coupled with hypotheticals (without attaching ourselves to the outcomes), we are building our "resilience muscle."

Fully committing ourselves to our actions is where the magic lies. Half measures really do avail you of nothing. Try to imagine a wedding proposal where a man says to his girlfriend, "Yeah, well, the divorce rate stinks, but if you're willing to give this marriage thing a shot, I'm game. …..So, do you wanna get married, or what?" Blerg. (My answer to that proposal would be "no," by the way).

When we are tethered to the past or connected to possible outcomes, we cannot live with resilience because we are relying on others to create our happiness. We are bound by our regret of what has passed or by fears of what is to come. We must learn to fully inhabit the present and be prepared (as best we can) to deal with what happens. Living in the present requires an agility and flexibility which is a natural byproduct of resilience.

Say aloud to yourself, "I am worthy of good things."

Chapter Eight
Yuk it Up, Fuzzball

Yes, I know that the title quote comes from Han Solo and Star Wars, but have any of you seen the Ron Howard film Splash? For the trivia buffs in the peanut gallery, it was the first movie I saw on a real date while in high school, but for the purposes of this book, it also provides a point of reference for today's exercise.

Professor Kornbluth, played by Second City alum Eugene Levy, has been in hot pursuit of Tom Hanks's onscreen love interest, Darryl Hannah, a mermaid who has come aground in New York City in search of Hanks. Absolutely no one believes that Kornbluth has identified a mermaid, and after a series of injuries trying to prove her existence, he takes a header – a particularly unpleasant tumble – down a stairwell. Out of the frame, at the foot of the stairs, we hear him bleat, "What a week I'm having."

When you're going through a crappy experience, in the words of my grandmother, "You can laugh or you can cry." I choose laughter, and here's why.

> "Laughter gives us distance. It allows us to step back from an event, deal with it and then move on." – Bob Newhart

While I have cried, do cry and believe in the cathartic nature of tears, I think laughter is sometimes a more potent tool in our arsenal when we need to act. Crying can present a slippery slope into self-pity, and depression that can bog us down. When we focus on the humor in any given situation, we automatically shift into a positive mindset. It's impossible to simultaneously laugh and be negative.

Sometimes, our laughter is reflexive. We laugh at ourselves from an awareness bigger and more acute than our conscious selves. Have you ever done something particularly idiotic (while alone) and then literally laughed out loud at yourself? I have. "Smooth move!" I'll chortle to myself, and then go about changing my behavior or trying another approach.

Laughter is good medicine; both our physical and mental health benefit when we laugh:

> Reduces pain. Our bodies produce pain-killing hormones called endorphins in response to laughter.
>
> Strengthens immune function. A good belly laugh increases production of T-cells, interferon and immune proteins called globulins.
>
> Decreases stress. When under stress, we produce a hormone called cortisol. Laughter significantly lowers cortisol levels and returns the body to a more relaxed state.

Aside from the increased flow of oxygen to our cells that laughter provides, I think it also helps us to relax, which allows for possibility thinking. Sometimes, we get so focused on a particular result that when we don't see our preferred specific outcome manifesting, we get wound up. Stressed out. Tense. Laughter is a natural purge valve that allows us to release expectations and open ourselves up to opportunities we haven't considered.

I actually keep a file of laughter-inducing YouTube clips in my bookmarks for those days when I don't find much to laugh about (they're mostly of babies, puppies and classic Simpsons scenes). Today, you may also wish to read a funny book or hang out with friends who make you laugh.

For extra credit: consider taking an improv class. Being around curious, hilarious people will help you to see things from a different perspective and enlarge your social circle as well. The more opportunities for intersections in your life, the greater your chance of serendipity having a chance to work its magic.

Say aloud to yourself, "I am worthy of good things."

Chapter Nine
Crank Up the Jams

Music is a sequence of spiritual vibrations that alters our moods, consciousness and realities. Pay attention to the music you choose for your environment. For example, I can only write when listening to classical music. Anything else distracts me. When cleaning the house, I choose upbeat tunes.

Be mindful of your music today. If you're feeling down, choose a soundtrack that reverses your mood. If you're tense, find something with soothing melodies. Experiment to find a type of music that helps to restore balance to your life.

> "Whatever meaning one chooses for spirituality, I believe there are direct correlations to each in the nature of music. Music is essential to human life and an integral part of our development as individuals and as a species. Like breath, music has rhythm, tension and release. One might even claim that the sound of breath, or the waves of the ocean are musical expressions of life.
>
> The beginning of the universe, according to modern science, was created by sound — the

Big Bang. The ancient myth of the goddess Voce claims that she created the world by singing it into existence. Few things in life have the ability to directly shape or shift our emotional state than music." – Frank Fitzpatrick, Grammy-nominated songwriter and producer

For some help in matching (or changing) your mood, check out the website www.//moodfuse.com.

For extra credit: create playlists with your favorites to keep on hand for those times when you need to change up your energy.

Say aloud to yourself, "I am worthy of good things."

CHAPTER TEN
Get Down and Dirty

Today, make plans to get some literal dirt under your nails. Whether you are a gardener or not, being exposed to the earth is good medicine. There's evidence that the composition of soil is beneficial to our mental health.

While you may not heard of a soil microbe called Mycobacterium vaccae, it has the power to shift your brain chemistry. It has been shown to trigger mouse brains to produce serotonin (thereby acting as an antidepressant). According to a study performed at the Sage Colleges in Troy, New York, mice exposed to it were shown to have less anxiety, learned better and ran through mazes faster and more competently.

If you don't have a garden, go to the park. Dig a bit in a space that has already been cultivated. Scoop up a bit of the good earth and smell it. Go to a conservatory. Hang out with the plants.

To get my green fix when I was a single mother and my daughters were young, we adopted a planter located downtown through a program sponsored by the chamber of commerce. We spent time planting and tending a patch of ground in the heart of the city. The girls had fun and we all enjoyed the time we spent together.

Also, consider this: you're not dead. You're dormant.

In Chicago, the landscape in the midwest is bleak and windswept during the winter. No vegetation grows and the trees are shut down for the season. As cliche as it sounds, when I'm wading through snow drifts on my way into the bus stop, spring (and its soft green, spongy new grass) seems a million months away. It's as though it will always be Winter.

Of course, this isn't true.

Sometimes we go through dormancies in our lives, but they can be more difficult to detect: Fallow periods where our productivity seems to plummet. Quarters where we post no new sales. If you're in the creative fields, writing, painting, composing or other artistic Muses seem to have taken a vacation, leaving our creativity to atrophy.

Whenever I think that I am not being productive or everything seems "bare" around me, I think of hydrangeas. If you've ever seen a dormant hydrangea, you know what I mean. It looks like a dried up bundle of sticks (and more than one gardener has mistakenly thought that the shrub in this state to be dead). Nope.

Not dead. Sleeping. Conserving energy. Planning for spring.

Hydrangeas need the season of dormancy to bloom and flourish. A friend of mine, who lives in Southern California, once sighed, "I wish I lived where you do so that I could grow hydrangeas in my garden." I laughed in response. This, from a woman who has bird of paradise that cost $12 a stem at my co-op clogging the meridian strips on her roadways. Perspective, huh?

Without our harsh and brutally cold winters, the hydrangea would never achieve dormancy. Therefore, the hydrangea bush literally cannot produce flowers without environmental adversity.

Unrelated to flowers, but related to dormancy, is a scene from The Princess Bride that always makes me laugh: It takes place in the hut of Miracle Max, who revives The Man in Black (Westley in disguise) from being mostly dead.

"'Mostly' dead is 'slightly alive,'" explains Miracle Max.

When you are experiencing dormancy, you are slightly alive. Focus on your strengths; take the long view to achieving your goals and stick with it.

For extra credit: start an indoor herb garden on your window sill. Tending the plants and watching the miracle of mute, brown earth release a neon green, tender shoot and nurturing it to wholeness will add to your quality of life in more than one way. I promise.

Say aloud to yourself, "I am worthy of good things."

Chapter Eleven
Hero Worship

Believe it or not, someone looks up to you. Before you laugh at my suggestion, ask yourself: is there someone you've always admired, but you've never told? A teacher, perhaps? Classmate? A babysitter? A brother or sister? A coworker?

The same holds true for someone else thinking that way about you.

I don't know why we are so shy about telling other people how much we admire them. It takes so little energy and yet generates such beneficial impact.

You can change that right now. Take a moment and write out two or three sentences to someone you admire, and tell him or her why. Fold up the paper and put it in an envelope. Pop it in the mail today. Bonus points if you use a fun stamp.

Writing and sending an email will also work, but there is something about putting pen to paper that makes a difference in our brain chemistry.

What you send out into the world returns to you. Karma knows your address, baby.

Say aloud to yourself, "I am worthy of good things."

Chapter Twelve
It's a Dog's Life

Dogs are good juju.

Unless you are allergic, today's assignment is hanging out with a dog. Owning a dog helps counter depression, along with a slew of other health benefits (including lowering blood pressure).

If you own a dog, spend some extra time with your four-legged friend today. Take him to the park; brush her coat. Tell him a story that you haven't told anyone else about what you'd like to do with your life.

Dogs listen.

I remember when I was at a low point in my marriage being able to just pour my guts out to our family's Shiba Inu. Miko was a furry little sponge who absorbed my sadness, and then we went for a walk and let it all just evaporate into the autumn air.

If you don't own a dog, consider volunteering at a shelter. Take a walk around the neighborhood and ask the dog owners you encounter if you may pet their doggo. If mobility is an issue, check out @dog_rates on twitter (https://twitter.com/dog_rates). This account is chock-full of heckin' cute puppers.

One of my habits when I'm out and about is to notice when I see a dog's head sticking out of a car window. Whenever I see their joyful, windblown faces, I remind myself, "Breathe. Chill. Be present. Enjoy the moment."

Dogs get it.

Say aloud to yourself, "I am worthy of good things."

CHAPTER THIRTEEN
The Metaphysics of Chocolate

Fernando Pessoa was on to something.

Scientifically proven to elevate your mood, chocolate is a fantastic treat that boosts your brain power and may protect your heart health. I am not talking about milk chocolate or white chocolate (which, as any pedant – like me – can tell you, technically isn't chocolate).

While I will have a square of milk chocolate occasionally, the true benefits of chocolate don't occur until you're eating high-octane dark chocolate. I actually refer to this as 'medicinal grade' chocolate only half in jest and have weaned myself to 85% dark.

At this level, the antioxidants in this magical bean can contribute to elevated mood, are a boon to your heart and carry many other physiological benefits. Chocolate packs a dense nutritional punch, which includes groovy goodness like this:

Iron

Copper

Magnesium

Zinc

Phosphorus

Flavanols (which sounds like a 50's doo-wop band)

I keep two of the Trader Joe's Dark Chocolate Lover's Chocolate bars in my pantry at all times (the one with the neon green package), and have a square or two every night. Once in awhile, I'll pair it with a glass of red wine (because antioxidants – better living through science, right?).

The secret here is to learn how to focus on quality and not quantity.

How much dime store chocolate are you consuming? How many empty, artificially-flavored, waxy calories are flowing through your bloodstream? Are you even tasting what you're eating? Do you savor chocolate, or mindlessly inhale it while rushing through your day? Pay attention. Choose wisely and with intention.

By paring down to the essential aspects of what is truly beneficial, you'll begin to lose your appetite for fillers (both literal and figurative), and you'll begin to gravitate toward what really feeds you. Watch how your life changes once you bring intention to seemingly small choices like this.

And all because of a magical brown bean. Pretty neat, huh?

Say aloud to yourself, "I am worthy of good things."

Chapter Fourteen
Good Morning, Starshine

When I was in college, I signed up for an Astronomy course. At the time of my registration, the subject was taught from an astrology perspective. In all honesty, I took it because I had a heavy course load that semester and thought that the class would be a respite from more intellectually taxing material.

Fate, it would seem, had other plans. As luck would have it, the Astronomy instructor had a family emergency happen during the winter break, and his replacement was a physicist whose approach to the material was radically different. The course content had switched from sun charts and the Zodiac to the science of nebulae and their stars' composition.

Yoinks!

As it turned out, Fate knew what it was doing.

The stars swirl, shine and dance within an immeasurable expanse of space. They've always fascinated me, and after having survived my college experience, I have a new appreciation for the presence of the universe in all life.

You really are stardust. Some believe that everything has an energetic signature – a coalescence of frequencies that gather in a specific alignment. You are a physical manifestation of an ancient, complex narrative that has written its story across the expanse of time.

>Boron
>
>Magnesium
>
>Copper
>
>Hydrogen
>
>Iron

These elements, and many others, are all present in the cells of your body. They fuel your movements, your thoughts and your dreams. Today's exercise? Go look at the stars. Lie on your back, relax all of your muscles, breathe deeply and contemplate the immensity you not only inhabit but represent.

Say aloud to yourself, "I am worthy of good things."

Chapter Fifteen
Take a Note

Pencils + paper = spiritual alchemy.

Full of possibility, your story lies dormant within this wood and graphite instrument. Start writing. Watch your higher self start to speak up (out?), and witness your life change.

Despite the advent of smartphones, tablets and texting, writing using long hand still has immense value.

While typing and other digital forms of communication have expanded the possibilities for communication, putting pen (or pencil) to paper contributes to your brain's capacity for elasticity, retention and forming cogent thoughts in a measurable way.

Multiple studies have shown the connection between writing and increased cognition, retention and creativity.

Journaling is an invaluable daily practice that can help you sift your subconscious. While I write every day, it can seem overwhelming for those who may be just starting new habits. This book has thrown a few habit adjustments at you already, and so even if only for today, let's write. If it becomes a daily habit, great; if not, consider keeping it among the tools in your toolbox.

I would encourage you to try to write for at least five minutes every day. Your topics can vary from random thoughts to working through a particular challenge you may be facing at any given moment. That said, for right now, take a moment to go get your notebook and a timer.

Pick just one of these topics and write about it for fifteen minutes:

I am happiest when…

My favorite thing about my life is…

Talking about _____ is difficult for me because…

I wish I had more _____ so that I could…

Don't worry if you spend a few minutes staring off into space before writing. It's part of the process. But stick with it for the entire fifteen minutes. Something will surface; I promise.

Some clues: the topic you chose indicates your higher self chiming in with its $.02 regarding your next life phase or iteration. We usually know what we need at a subconscious level before our day-to-day operating systems catch up (or are willing to acknowledge).

If anything filtered to the surface that affects you strongly, consider pursuing it by adding it to your daily journaling or meditation routine. Now put your writing materials away for the day, stretch and congratulate yourself.

Good work!

Say aloud to yourself, "I am worthy of good things."

Chapter Sixteen
Tug o'war vs. Hug o'war

Hug O' War is one of my favorite poems from the book, Where the Sidewalk Ends: the poems & drawings of Shel Silverstein. I like his poetry in general, but this poem reminds me that touch and physical contact is an essential part of our overall health as human beings.

There are many health benefits related to hugging, whether you are being hugged or giving one. For instance, when we hug someone, oxytocin is released into our bodies by our pituitary gland, lowering both our heart rates and our cortisol levels. Cortisol is the hormone responsible for stress, high blood pressure, and heart disease.

So if you're not around people who will hug you, find them. In lieu of hugs, consider massage or reflexology. Or get a manicure or pedicure today. Touch is important.

Say aloud to yourself, "I am worthy of good things."

CHAPTER SEVENTEEN
How to Find Your Purpose

We came into this world tethered at the navel and we've been gazing at it ever since.

> "Why are we here?"
>
> "Why were we born?"
>
> "What does it mean?"
>
> "How did it start?"
>
> "Where do I end?"
>
> "What is my purpose?"

From the time we show up on this planet and the interval of years between before our exit, most of us meander around this rock wondering what it's all about and what we're supposed to do. The few of us who have, for whatever reason, honed into their purpose early on in the process seem to have the greatest effect on the rest of us, regardless of their industry or discipline.

Dubbed geniuses all, their sense of purpose provided an overarching and guiding element to their endeavors. Having a purpose is an amazing sort of high octane rocket fuel that guides and propels your life.

I stumbled across this exercise about four years ago, and it has provided a cosmic yardstick against which I measure ninety-five percent of the efforts I have expended subsequently.

How to discover your life purpose in about 20 minutes.

Take out a blank sheet of paper or open up a word processor where you can type.

Write at the top, "What is my true purpose in life?"

Write an answer (any answer) that pops into your head. It doesn't have to be a complete sentence. A short phrase is fine.

Repeat step 3 until you write the answer that makes you cry. This is your purpose.

© Steve Pavlina

Two things:

1. It works.
2. Your life will never be the same.

Once you've determined your purpose, you can never go back to your life as it was before. There are a few things you can focus on with your journaling in order to leverage and employ this newfound wisdom to its best effect.

Where do you want your life to go?

Where do your interests, talents and purpose overlap or align?

How will you begin to sketch out your map or blueprint to reach your destination?

Who will need to be on your team or in your orbit?

As you explore these action items, check them against your gut feeling. Your core has an unnameable wisdom that we have yet to quantify in the conscious realm. In order to hear your intuition, you must learn how to silence the world on a daily basis.

By this point, if you've been following along with the exercises in the book, you will have probably developed a discipline to focus your energy for twenty minutes. During these twenty minutes, literally spend the time concentrating on breathing. Once you've gotten good at centering yourself and wiping the mental slate clean, start to introduce the above questions about your purpose and how best to fulfill it.

The answers will filter to the top of your awareness as if by magic.

Once you've begun the process of determining your purpose, you will find that others who wish to help you will come out of the woodwork. I don't know why, but my life experience has shown me that there is a personal polarity that occurs when you begin to live out your purpose, drawing resources and individuals to you who share in your vision.

Another promise: you will never encounter anything for which you do not have the tools/skills to handle or process. Never. Ever. Anything that comes your way once you've determined your purpose is spiritual calisthenics. Working through these calisthenics is how you cultivate your resilience muscle(s).

While your mileage may vary, again; I have found it to be true that distilling one's purpose activates a possibility magnet that helps provide resources and tools for the next stages of your journey.

That's it. Paper, pen, or keyboard and Word doc – whatever it takes. Your answers will come.

Have you found your purpose? How? How has it changed your life? Where has it led you? Is your life now what you expected it would be? Please share your story with me – send me an email. Your response may find its way into a future book, or I may send you a reply through social media.

Say aloud to yourself, "I am worthy of good things."

Chapter Eighteen
Get Bent

When I was a little girl, I used to watch Lilias, Yoga and You on PBS, hosted by Lilias M. Folan with my grandmother. She and I would wear our leotards and bend all over the living room while stretched out in front of our television.

Yoga can seem intimidating to those who assume that spendy leggings and expensive doo-dads are required in order to practice this ancient discipline. They aren't. If you have a body, you can do yoga.

    Breathing.

    Mindfulness.

    Flexibility.

    Awareness.

    Balance.

    Oxygen.

    Focus.

These are the elements of yoga that are necessary in order to conduct a daily practice. You can even do yoga at your desk while at the office.

Today, your assignment is to do perform these three basic yoga poses:

> The Corpse Pose. This is literally lying on your back. Focus on releasing the tension in your body as you let gravity do the work.
>
> The Upward Salute. Inhale and sweep your arms overhead in wide arcs. If your shoulders are tight, keep your hands apart and gaze straight ahead. Otherwise, bring your palms together, drop your head back, and gaze up at your thumbs.
>
> Viparita Karani (Legs Up the Wall Pose). It's okay if your legs make a little triangle between you and the wall. You may not be able to have your legs flat against the wall the first time you do this. Do not force anything.

The most important thing with yoga is to pay attention to your body and your breath. Do not force your body to go beyond its present capability or capacity. Pain is not gain here. If you pick these three poses and do them every day, you will increase your range of motion and flexibility. You will expand your lung capacity. You will learn how to center and align your body and mind.

As you get stronger, you may wish to add more poses. Or not. Although I do yoga every day, I am not a buff yogi. I am a flexible fifty-one year old who can squat down on the floor next to a two-year old for extended periods of time. My goal is flexibility, elasticity, stress management and mindfulness.

You may choose to expand your yoga practice to be more athletic. But the three poses given are the bare minimum of accessible poses for pretty much any body. The standard disclaimer applies. I am not a doctor. Before you begin any fitness program, talk with your doctor to determine a course of what's best for you.

Say aloud to yourself, "I am worthy of good things."

Chapter Nineteen
Mind Your Manners

At their essence, manners are the recognition and respect of self in other. When we use good manners, we are actually acknowledging our own worthiness of being treated well and with respect. In so saying, I of course realize that not everyone practices good manners. There are many rude (and psychologically wounded) people walking the planet.

Whenever you choose to act in a kind and mannerly way, you are saying to yourself and to others that you respect yourself.

Today, consciously choose to act in the mannerly way when interacting with your fellow humans.

> Say thank you
>
> Say you're welcome
>
> Hold the door open for others
>
> Offer your seat on the subway to someone who looks as though (s)he could use it
>
> Let someone off the elevator before you step in

Apologize when you are wrong

When you encounter someone who is rude, do not answer their rudeness with rudeness. Instead, let it go. Do not take it personally. If you would like, send them a silent thought of kindness, asking Whomever (God, Source, the Universe, the Flying Spaghetti Monster etc.) to intervene on their behalf.

When you shift your attitude to a position of grace, you will experience grace in return. Random kindnesses will be extended to you. Your stress levels will go down. I have personally experienced this state of "good luck," by the way. Even when things go "poorly" for me, I have found that my fall is always broken by grace.

Practicing manners and kindness will develop your resilience rapidly.

Say aloud to yourself, "I am worthy of good things."

Chapter Twenty
Splish Splash

One of my favorite quotes is Isak Dinesen's "The cure for anything is salt water — sweat, tears, or the sea." I never knew that I needed to live next to water until a (blessedly brief) time in my life when I lived in a land-locked area. I grew up next to the Mississippi River and took it for granted. Living in an area that wasn't close to water was really stressful for me.

Now that I live in Chicago, there are many days when I head straight for the lake and just watch the waves roll in – even during the winter time. Listening to the sound of waves crashing on the shore lowers my stress levels immediately.

But what can you do if you don't live next to a body of water?

I made a reference to the humble Epsom salt bath earlier in the prologue. Something as simple as a soak in a hot bath can make a huge difference in your mindset. My evidence is anecdotal – the science on Epsom salts is still out – but if it helps you, in my opinion, then it's a good thing.

There are many days when a good soak in the tub is good for what ails me. Today's assignment is to find some water and reflect on how it makes you feel.

Say aloud to yourself, "I am worthy of good things."

Chapter Twenty-One
"I get by with a little help from my friends." – The Beatles

Writing this book has given a chance to review my relationships and people whose lives have intersected with mine. Your friends fall into different categories, with most of them joining you on your journey for a season or a segment of your life. Very few people have life-long friends, and that's okay.

Friends appear in our lives as mirrors or support for our own growth. You may have a group of friends who provide a sounding board for child rearing. You may have a group of friends at work who can help navigate the exciting world of office politics. Being part of a group of people experiencing the same struggles and challenges can be a life saver.

Of my friends, there is one woman who crosses my mind frequently. Her personality was an amazing combination of class and crass: manicured nails coupled with a sailor's mouth. She had a huge heart and a sparkling wit.

She went to the hospital one day because her throat hurt, and she couldn't figure out what was wrong. The doctors identified cancer in her lymph nodes that day, and she died four months later. She never left the hospital.

Four months. A blip. A season. She never saw it coming. I don't wish to be a Debbie Downer, but one of the best lessons I took away from my friendship with her was to live big; laugh often and love fully.

How about you? Do you have examples of friends who have helped you grow? Today's exercise is to grab your notebook and take a moment to list some of the friends who have taught you lessons over the years. Now add to the list the friends who are currently in your orbit.

Do you have some friends that you've outgrown? Are there "frenemies" in your circle of acquaintances? Make sure that the people you allow into your world are people who love you, support you and encourage you to develop your highest self.

My goal here isn't to tell you to dump your friends. But if your goal in picking up this book is to change your brain (and by extension, your life), be sure that you are choosing your friends wisely.

In a pair of studies involving nearly 280,000 people, William Chopik, assistant professor of psychology at Michigan State University, also found that friendships become increasingly important to one's happiness and health across the lifespan.

"Friendships become even more important as we age," says Chopik. "Keeping a few really good friends around can make a world of difference for our health and well-being. So it's smart to invest in the friendships that make you happiest."

So take another look at your list of friends. Which ones help you grow? Which ones drain you? Where can you go today that puts you in the path of others who share your interests?

Finally, make sure that you are being a good friend to yourself. Be mindful of your self talk. Make sure you are feeding yourself foods that nourish you. Get some sleep when you need it.

Say aloud to yourself, "I am worthy of good things."

Chapter Twenty-Two
Bust a Move

Cut a rug. Have you ever watched a toddler dance? They have an innate response to music that tends to fade at some point for most of us in our lives. Toddlers do that little boop boop, knee bounce sway when they hear a tune that moves them.

Not only is it adorable, it's also a reminder that we were born to dance.

I dance in my kitchen, and I dance while using my standing desk (impromptu dance parties are the best part of having a standing desk). The quote "dance like no one's watching" exists for a reason. Music liberates. Music energizes. Tap into the power of tunes.

Today, your assignment is to dance in your kitchen.

For extra credit: sign up for a dance class. You never know who you'll meet when dancing cheek to cheek.

Say aloud to yourself, "I am worthy of good things."

Chapter Twenty-Three
Paradox is a Hoot

If you're familiar with Charles Dickens's book "A Tale of Two Cities, you'll recognize the reference of this Chapter. The full quote reads like this:

> "It was the best of times, it was the worst of times, it was the age of wisdom, it was the age of foolishness, it was the epoch of belief, it was the epoch of incredulity, it was the season of Light, it was the season of Darkness, it was the spring of hope, it was the winter of despair, we had everything before us, we had nothing before us, we were all going direct to Heaven, we were all going direct the other way—in short, the period was so far like the present period, that some of its noisiest authorities insisted on its being received, for good or for evil, in the superlative degree of comparison only."

Paradox is an invitation to examine where you are in life and to look for the lesson it holds. A quick glance into your past will probably reveal times of true misery: stretches of bad luck or losses that brought you to your knees. And yet, along those same stretches, you can probably identify glimpses of grace and kindness that revealed blessings you may not have otherwise seen.

Today, please jot down in your notebook your worst memory. What about it was unpleasant? How did you transition from this event or period of your life? What were the bright spots and lessons that you took away from it? Being able to identify and process these memories is proof that you're a survivor.

Now take a moment to write down your best memory.

What about it resonates? Where was the joy? Quiet your mind and try to determine what, specifically, about this memory makes you happy. By recalling these details, you are recreating the event. You are also helping to identify opportunities for you to generate these positive opportunities in your present and future lives while avoiding the painful repeats of those memories that gave you lessons.

Say aloud to yourself, "I am worthy of good things."

CHAPTER TWENTY-FOUR
Take a Grass Bath

When was the last time you walked across your front lawn in your bare feet? Most of us spend our days with our feet confined to shoe prisons, releasing them only occasionally to the relative freedom of trapping them in the softer shackles of socks.

Today, your task is to walk through some fresh, green grass. Find a park or other green space if you don't live in a rural or suburban environment. Take the time to really connect with the feeling of cool, spoingy, new grass under your bare feet.

If you have the time and opportunity, upgrade your grassy experiment by taking a leisurely stroll in a wooded area. The Japanese refer to this as "green bathing," and it has been shown to generate significant health benefits.

Make it a habit to be around green at least three times a week.

Say aloud to yourself, "I am worthy of good things."

Chapter Twenty-Five
Pay It Forward

Today's exercise is twofold. For the entire day, focus on others who are expressing kindness and extend kindness as well. Opportunities to flex this:

> Don't interrupt anyone.
>
> Hold the door open for someone else.
>
> Pay for the coffee or parking of the person behind you.
>
> Make eye contact at the check out.
>
> Help a stranger with directions.
>
> Give a sincere compliment.
>
> Buy a candy bar from the kid at the subway entrance.
>
> Give a homeless person some cash.

Go through your contacts list and make introductions between people.

Let someone cut in line ahead of you.-

This list is just a beginning. For additional ideas, a simple Google search for "random acts of kindness" will generate hundreds of ideas for being the kindness you wish to see in the world.

For the second portion of today's exercise, grab your notebook. Take a moment and think of the times in your life when someone else's kindness made a difference to you. Perhaps it was a teacher who gave you the benefit of the doubt on an essay question. Maybe it was a police officer who gave you a warning instead of a ticket that would have strained your budget (or wreaked havoc with your car insurance).

Really meditate on the impact that kindness has had on your life and vow to pay it forward. Karma works (and it also pays dividends).

There are people who go out of their way to do kind things for other people. They're out there. We're out here. Want proof? To learn more about how they work, check out the site for Random Acts of Kindness:

www.raok.org

Say aloud to yourself, "I am worthy of good things."

CHAPTER TWENTY-SIX
Nothing Ventured; Nothing Gained

Most of us have gotten used to the relative safety of routine or a life lived to satisfy others' expectations. How many of you identify yourself through a role you play (whether as someone's parent or through your job or career)? There is a small but important distinction between quantifying what you do for a living and what you feel your identity to be.

For example: as a mother, I notice that many of my peers find themselves without their moorings once their children graduate high school and move 'out of the nest.' Their entire life and center has been defined as being adjacent to and supportive of someone else. I love my daughters more than I can say, but it's possible to be a supportive parent without subsuming or conflating your worth into the whole of another's existence.

There are others reading this book who may be graduating from college right now with a degree for a discipline of study that they hate. Perhaps the family pinned their hopes on having someone in the family with a law degree and you may have yearned to pursue botany instead? Yet here you sit with a freshly minted piece of parchment (and the debt that goes with it), ready to start your life, living someone else's ideal.

> "Until you learn to name your ghosts and to baptize your hopes, you have not yet been born, you are still the creation of others." – Marie Cardinal

Today's exercise is all about naming your ghosts and baptizing your hopes. Starting off your life's journey saddled with thousands of dollars of debt, staring down endless years of professional torture, seen in black and white terms, is not something most people would choose, and yet when we live our lives, it's more difficult to recognize in practice.

Our roles are established early, whether through birth order, our resemblance to a relative, our parent's marriage or lack of a spouse... for example:

Your expectation may be that the eldest son inherits the family business.

Since your namesake was a lawyer, you're expected to become one.

You may have been the baby of the family, and expected to be wild and outrageous.

You may have been the only boy in a family of mostly women and raised within strict gender norms.

Perhaps you were a girl and taught that your future was to be a stay-at-home mom.

You may have gotten a job early in your teen years and expected to contribute to the family's finances.

While none of these is 'wrong,' on its own, per se, (e.g. you may very well be the oldest son whose dream it is to inherit the family business, or you love being a wife and mother), if your reality doesn't align with your dreams and aptitudes for yourself, you may find yourself either unhappy or operating below your potential.

That being said, we must do the heavy lifting to divest ourselves of others' expectations and assumptions of us if we are to become an authentic person. This is really difficult to do and usually painful at first. Honestly, I can't tell you how or where it starts. But recognition of your need to become yourself is the first step toward resilience.

Being willing to start over represents the beginning of this process. Not everyone is willing to take this risk. Give yourself credit for honoring your willingness to do so. It's significant, and a success in and of itself. Congratulations!

In terms of self-awareness, I can't tell you what comes first, awareness of self or the knowledge that there's a better way. The best advice I can give to you is that if you are feeling anything other than excitement and joy about your life or future, pause and ask yourself, "What do I want?" and "Why am I unhappy?"

Ask yourself these questions while driving down the road; while mowing the lawn; doing the dishes; riding on the subway – whenever it is that you've identified your brain is on standby mode. This is the time when your subconscious is usually at the wheel. Then listen for the answer(s). Once you have an inkling that you want something different, now you are ready to throw your life into a season of chaos.

The good news? It's worth it. Ready to play along?

> "The creation of something new is not accomplished by the intellect but by the play instinct acting from inner necessity. The creative mind plays with the objects it loves." – Carl Jung

For me, Jung's quote means that we don't think our way out of pain, we play our way out of pain. Secondly, and most important, we ourselves are the object we love.

In order to change our lives for the better, we must believe that we deserve something better. We must understand that living a complete and vibrant life is a necessity. So many of us postpone fulfillment of our potential or dreams because we think that it's a luxury, or it's something that we can concentrate on after 1. the kids graduate 2. we get a better job 3. ...get married. …. 4. Some undefined artificial and ephemeral yardstick. It's not. It's now. You deserve it.

By play, I understand that to mean that we are to make of our challenges a game. Considering "what ifs" and experimentation is how we learn. It's how we learned as children. For example, how many of us looked at a bicycle and drew out the angles of declination, stepped on a scale to determine our weight, configured the formula for velocity, mass and inertia before hopping on the banana seat and tearing off around the corner? Probably one. Maybe two of you. More than likely, none of you. Instead, you got hopped up on sugar, slung your leg over the bar and started pedaling, hitting the pavement and skinning a knee or two along the way. Same difference here.

Once you've identified opportunities and means to change, take a big, deep breath and pick a figurative cement piling in the foundation of your life. Then pick up a sledgehammer and start swinging:

What goes first?

> Is it a habit?
>
> Is it a job?
>
> Is it the people you choose to surround yourself with?

Trust your gut and go with the one you know you can commit to and complete. This act will begin the metamorphosis that will result in the evolution of you as an authentic, vibrant being. (Spoiler alert: you're never done. You are now, in the words of filmmaker Melissa Pierce, in a state of perpetual beta).

Acceptance of this fact will paradoxically allow you to relax and really enjoy your life – even the scary parts. For what it's worth, although I truly believe that once you clue in to the fact that you are an evolving being, you will never be "done," I can also say that (based on my own experiences) segue portions, or transition periods, of my life occur across two-year increments.

There's only so much tensile strength our corporeal shells possess and can process within the carbon-based restrictions we're working with on this plane. While the soul is infinite, the construct into which it is placed has many variables (i.e. other people's timelines, your own ability to process, the price of tea in China, etc.). That's why we get a lifetime to practice.

Today's exercise: While you're hip deep in life rubble, take time to draft the blueprint of what you desire for yourself. Through the power of your imagination, you become the architect of your life. While operating within this framework, you can plug yourself in to various scenarios:

Self as pilot.

Self as chef.

Self as physicist.

Self as cosmetologist.

Spend a few minutes in your notebook to jot down a blueprint of your desired future. Identify some of the gut reactions that have filtered to the surface. Which ones excite you? Think about what you already have that can create this future. Be open to attracting the remaining resources and tools from a yet-unknown source.

It's very simple, but that doesn't mean that it's easy.

Say aloud to yourself, "I am worthy of good things."

Chapter Twenty-Seven
Oil Be There for You

I swear by aromatherapy. Scientifically speaking, the sense of smell anchors memories into your brain's hard drive. According to multiple studies cited by Yale Scientific, the olfactory system is the only sensory system that involves the amygdala and the limbic system in its primary processing pathway. This link explains why smells are often linked to specific memories. For example, if you have had a positive experience while being in a coffee shop, the scent of coffee may induce positive thoughts.

Expanded claims about the healing properties of essential oils may or may not have a scientific basis, but anecdotally, I can tell you that my moods are improved by using different scents for various reasons.

Have you ever …reacted positively to the smell of a freshly-peeled orange or the sliced lemons used to garnish your iced tea? …crushed rosemary leaves in between your fingers and been able to smell the scent of the plant on your hand? …rubbed a basil leaf before making caprese salad?

All of these are instances of tuning into the primal force of scent in order to alter your mood.

Today, your task is to go to the nearest drug or department store and buy a few drams of essential oil. For a guide, here are some common commercially-available essential oils and their properties:

    Lavender – Calming, relaxing

    Frankincense – Meditative, grounding, calming

    Peppermint – Uplifting, invigorating

    Eucalyptus – Clarifying

    Tea Tree – Cleansing, purifying

    Grapefruit – Uplifting, refreshing

    Rosemary – Uplifting, energizing, purifying

    Lemon – Uplifting, cleansing, freshening

    Sweet Orange – Uplifting, cleansing, freshening

    Patchouli – Grounding, relaxing

    Bergamot – Uplifting, energizing, purifying

    Lemongrass – Uplifting, cleansing, purifying

I keep a roller ball tube of essential oils in my handbag during the day. It comes in handy when I'm on the train and faced with the smells of the city. Or I'll apply a few drops to my palm and apply pressure to the muscles between my thumb and forefinger to help with the onset of a headache. If I'm having difficulty sleeping, I'll apply lavender oil to the soles of my feet. There are many ways to use essential oils to contribute to your sense of well being.

Adding essential oils to a bath, or to a sachet for your closet are other ways to incorporate the impact of scent in your environment. Experiment with different combinations. See what works best for you.

Say aloud to yourself, "I am worthy of good things."

Chapter Twenty-Eight
Channel Your Inner George Bailey

Most of us are familiar with the Frank Capra film, It's a Wonderful Life, starring James Stewart as the suicidal small town lender from Bedford Falls that airs around the Christmas season. It is only after the intervention of a mulled wine enthusiast and Angel, Second Class Clarence Odbody, who reveals to Stewart's George Bailey what world without him would have been like, that George appreciates the incredible life he has had.

The film culminates with the famous scene of essentially the entire town dropping by the Bailey residence and throwing cash into a basket to help replace the money stolen by local baddie and slumlord Henry F. Potter. As his beaming family is gathered around him, George is toasted by his younger brother, returning war hero, Harry, who says, "A toast! ...to my big brother George: The richest man in town."

Today's exercise is to list all of the ways your life intersects with others in a positive fashion, from the biggest to the most seemingly insignificant. You will be missed. It's based in science: nature abhors a vacuum. If you're not here, your spot in the universe folds in on itself. Your absence sets in motion a domino effect of loss.

Some suggestions of the folks who may cross your path:

> A barista who remembers your order?
>
> Kids at a school where you volunteer as a reader?
>
> A new-hire at work who relies on your mentorship?
>
> A bus driver who smiles when they see you?
>
> A neighbor who shares veggies from her garden with you over the backyard fence?

Each of these connections weaves the web of your life. If you have the time, consider all of the ways that your interactions has had an impact on another's life.

And now I encourage you to flip the switch again: are there people in your life who have told you how much they appreciate you? I call this my "cheerleader file," and it has changed my mood more than once. When my perspective is skewed by my doubt, I take the time to go through these messages and mementos sent to me from people whose lives I have touched for the better.

These saved messages remind me that I matter – that what I do makes a difference. These "atta girl" messages are from people who see the best in me and remind me of my better nature when I've sometimes forgotten. They reinforce the idea that I have a chance to become the person I'm capable of becoming, and isn't that what we strive for in our quest for resilience? To be reminded that we can 'bounce back'?"

Evolving into who we can be and developing our potential is a scary and sacred journey. Thank goodness we don't have to go it alone.

For extra credit, here's a one more exercise for today: this is going to sound counter intuitive, but I'm going to ask you to pay attention to the troubles of people around you. When you go through the checkout line at the grocery store, pay attention to the gestures and facial expression of the person wearing the name tag standing across the counter from you.

He may have just $15 to last through the end of the week.

She may be worried about a goof up she just made at work.

He may have just heard that his mom was diagnosed with cancer.

She may be working her way through school and still have to study when her shift ends.

Take a moment, look them squarely in the eye and compliment them. A sincere one. Do this for one solid day with everyone you meet – cabbies, bosses, peers, children. Then reflect on the way you feel when you go to sleep that night. Write it down in your notebook or otherwise record it.

Try it again for the remainder of the week. Watch magical things happen in your life. This isn't woo-woo karma voodoo. This is social physics. Ripples are ripples, even if they are invisible. Just because I can't see electricity doesn't mean that I can't see its effects.

I'd be interested in hearing your responses to how this experiment worked for you. Please send me an email with your results. I may include your experiences in a future book or send a reply your way on social media.

Say aloud to yourself, "I am worthy of good things."

Chapter Twenty-Nine
Orange You Glad ?

When I moved to Chicago, I noticed that I gravitated to the color orange, using it for furnishings, throw pillows and linens throughout my apartment. Orange symbolizes energy, vitality, cheer, excitement, adventure, warmth, and good health. In retrospect, I find it interesting that these are the feelings needed to start over in a new town. Perhaps my subconscious was my interior decorator?

Color theory, in general, fascinates me. Have you ever considered the subliminal effects of color on mood? What you wear, the color of your bedroom or even the colors of the food you eat all contribute to your environment. Colors are a literal representation of frequencies and vibrations across a spectrum and have a different impact on everyone.

A quick Google search focusing on the meaning and impact of colors will yield insights that can help you decide what may work best for you if you'd like to change up your mood. Here are some brief summaries of the symbolism and meanings behind basic colors, according to Color Wheel Pro:

Red is the color of fire and blood, so it is associated with energy, war, danger, strength, power, determination as well as passion, desire, and love.

Orange combines the energy of red and the happiness of yellow, and represents enthusiasm, fascination, happiness, creativity, determination, attraction, success, encouragement, and stimulation.

Yellow is the color of sunshine. It's associated with joy, happiness, intellect, and energy. Yellow produces a warming effect, arouses cheerfulness, stimulates mental activity, and generates muscle energy.

Green is the color of nature. It symbolizes growth, harmony, freshness, and fertility. Green has strong emotional correspondence with safety.

Blue is the color of the sky and sea. It is often associated with depth and stability. It symbolizes trust, loyalty, wisdom, confidence, intelligence, faith, truth, and heaven.

Purple combines the stability of blue and the energy of red. Purple is associated with royalty. It symbolizes power, nobility, luxury, and ambition. It conveys wealth and extravagance. Purple is associated with wisdom, dignity, independence, creativity, mystery, and magic.

White is associated with light, goodness, innocence, purity, and virginity. It is considered to be the color of perfection. White means safety, purity, and cleanliness.

Black is associated with power, elegance, formality, death, evil, and mystery.

Take a look at your closet. Is there a dominant color? Does it make you feel cheerful? Depressed? Focus on your instinctive response.

If you live in an apartment and painting the walls isn't an option, consider using inexpensive fabric to create artwork – you can stretch it across frames you buy at the thrift shop. Changing your linens or using throw pillows are also easy ways to bring color into your life.

Once you're out and about, take a moment to really look at the blue sky, or the green leaves. Soak up the colors that surround you, and take the time to appreciate the ability to see them.

Say aloud to yourself, "I am worthy of good things."

Chapter Thirty
Daydream Believer – Channeling Your Woo Woo Katchoo

Your ability to imagine is one of the most underutilized powers we humans have. Everyone from sports heroes like Serena Williams and Michael Phelps to actors like Jim Carrey and Oprah Winfrey harness the power of visualization and imagination to develop resilience and fuel their future.

Here's a mind-bender poem you can reference for today's exercise:

> Join death
>
> to your life and you will live
>
> as if there were no drum to march to.
>
> There is no march at all.
>
> You're done. All will be well for all.
>
> – from All That's Left by Jack Hirschman

This chapter is pretty "woo woo" and "out there," but if you'll bear with me, I think you'll enjoy the detour. Over the past year, the idea of surrender as liberation has been bouncing around my head and I don't know where it will all end up. So if you'll bear with me, let's take a trip down the rabbit hole together.

Paradox is one of my life lessons that I'm supposed to learn as I navigate my journey. It took me about forty years to realize that fact, but since then, I've been practicing awareness of paradox for a few years, so it has become easier to recognize when I encounter it.

Most of the time, paradox is one of those intangible concepts – the truth of which is tucked in so deeply to the problem that the solution (or resolution) dangles just out of reach of our consciousness.

It's a Möbius Strip of awareness that chases itself right back into the hidden recesses of our consciousness, and can be exceedingly frustrating for Type A personalities like mine, who prefer more direct and explicit communications from the Universe (or God, Source, Flying Spaghetti Monster etc.). However, it is through our seeking that we find ourselves. It is always an inside job, so get used to the puzzle your life represents.

The really frustrating part of the journey is that once the tumblers do click and you comprehend the inherent paradox of whatever specific situation in which you find yourself, it is maddeningly difficult to explain to someone else. It's usually a lesson that is intensely personal. You just know.

How can we die yet live?

In the case of the poem's excerpt above, how does dying to our life free us? Is it freedom from expectations? Is it freedom from earthly concerns? Is it the figurative death of relationship or habit? Is it allowing us to focus on eternal matters?

As I mentioned above, most people (including yours truly) are more comfortable with clear cut beginnings and ends. For example:

> Articulate goal.
>
> Write it down.
>
> Take steps to achieve it.
>
> Achieve stated goal... and finally (in football parlance), move the chains.
>
> Repeat as necessary.

However, consider this: What if linear and nonlinear paths coexist simultaneously? What if the linear model of goal achieving outlined in the previous paragraph is absolutely correct? Or what if a random pathway would bring you to the same end? Is one more real or correct than the other? But wait. There's more – what if your path is at once independent and interrelated to every other path? What if all of the above are true? Would it matter?

As I see it, our responsibility to ourselves and each other is to tend our own garden. Set our own goals. Discern our own truths and live them out as best we can with what we have at any given time, reaching out to others who are able and willing to help us grow. In so doing, the betterment of the whole is advanced.

When we focus on our own skills, talents and the expression of same, we find that our lives are like an instrument playing within a symphony of humanity. Each life has a different tone, frequency, vibrancy and melody and yet each blends with the others when lived in an authentic manner.

> There is no march at all.

This sentiment is inherently annoying for most people, including me, because it is the opposite of all we hold dear. There must be some meaning to this, right? Because if there's not, then why are we here?

> It doesn't matter.

Boing! Has your brain bent yet? Perhaps the scale is so big that it's beyond our comprehension. Perhaps the realization of our ability and capacity to opt out of expectations is, in and of itself, the goal. Perhaps that's an enlightenment of sorts. I do know that embracing the paradox of surrender is liberating. However, there is a subtle difference between surrender and giving up.

Surrender is an acknowledgement that you've reached the limits of your comprehension. Giving up is not looking any farther. Once we surrender, we are open to new horizons; and that's where our resilience lies.

Today's exercise is to read this chapter again and to scribble a few of your thoughts about it that surface. Send me an email. You may be featured in a future book, or I may tweet out a response.

Say aloud to yourself, "I am worthy of good things."

Chapter Thirty-One
Grandma's Ghost

My grandmother taught me a lot as it relates to wisdom and life lessons in general. After my mom and dad divorced, my mom moved back in with her mother. Most of my formative childhood memories were forged with my grandmother serving a major part.

Grandma graduated from high school in 1932 and married shortly thereafter. My bedroom was her former sewing room, and the walls were adorned with family portraits, among them, her wedding picture. My grandfather was tall and lanky – all angles and ears. My grandmother stood as a soft, slender ivory column next to him. Her pin curls and Clara Bow pout stand out in my memory, especially. She was so young and hopeful.

Of course, in the 1930s, most of the world was experiencing The Great Depression. Global financial markets had tanked; the Great Dust Bowl had ravaged the topsoil of the midwest ...and yet among this hardship, she and my grandfather set out to begin their life together.

It wasn't until after she died that I found her wedding shoes: sinewy and chalk-like. The ghost of my grandmother spoke to me through these shoes, curled with age and cracked at the stress points where her foot would have flexed when she walked.

They were brown shoes that she had painted white, to match her wedding dress.

In this time of poverty, innovation and thrift inspired her first exercise of resilience.

One of the things of which I am most proud about my grandmother is that she did not weather the financial storm of the Great Depression with a sense of privation. Instead, she drew from the experience the reverse: how to celebrate what she had and to expand its possibilities through resourcefulness and creativity.

Her shoes now sit on a bookshelf in my dining room, a constant reminder of sacrifice, resilience and hope that anything can be borne, as long as you keep your heart from despair. Through the crucible of The Great Depression, she learned how to flex her creativity – a trait she passed on to her six children and twenty-four grandchildren.

As we go through life, it's easy to fall into the trap of thinking that we don't have enough resources, forgetting that we ourselves are our best source of renewal. Trust your vision. Nurture it. Flex your creativity and watch your resilience grow.

Today's exercise is to list an inventory of all your gifts and resources in your handy dandy notebook. Scan the list once you've written it, and choose one thing among them to put into practice today.

Say aloud to yourself, "I am worthy of good things."

Chapter Thirty-Two
Hearing vs. Listening

There's a saying that in order to learn, we must listen more and to speak less: Two ears and one mouth dictating the ratio of listening to speaking. There are many life lessons that are taught to us from other people, to whom we must listen.

For example, when I hear the same thing coming from two or more people within a short amount of time, that's a cosmic hint to me: I am being sent a message. Has this been your experience?

Many of us are poor listeners. Are you someone who, instead of listening to the person across the table from you, spends that time composing your reply? On occasion, I have been guilty of this transgression. Irish lineage and my natural tendencies have conspired to make me a chatterbox. Birth order (oldest of three) and general know-it-all-ness gave me a handicap of presuming that I already knew the answers to most questions. Thankfully, I have realized that there are a great many things I have yet to learn, and learning how to listen to others has cultivated my own powers of resilience much faster as a result.

Life and its attendant experiences have trained me to listen. When we are busy talking, we cannot hear. When we formulate our response to what we think is being said instead of what is actually being said, miscommunication and (possibly) misery may follow.

It is essential that we quiet our inner dialogue and focus on what the other is saying. There is a world of knowledge stored in the heads of others.

When I was a little kid, I can remember looking out the window of our family car as we made our way along the interstate during family trips. As I would watch other cars and trucks pass, I can remember thinking that each vehicle represented another family; another reality, distinct and different from mine.

In a similar fashion, every person we meet has an entirely different perspective, based upon his or her experiences to date. Their lives inform their decisions, their opinions and of course, their words.

When we take the time to truly listen to others, we can expand our own worlds through hearing their words.

Expansion and resilience forms the underpinning of the universe, really. Although there is an ebb and flow to all natural patterns, the cumulative effect is one of forward progression. Listening generates the same kind of social physics, in my opinion.

When we are around people who listen to us, our world expands. We are encouraged to explore our inner landscape and to develop the vision we find there. By speaking it aloud, we give form and shape to our ideas.

I was able to actually witness this effect once, when a friend shared with me a dream that had percolating in her mind. Although this idea had been sifting in her head for quite some time, speaking it aloud (and in the presence of others) gave her idea a concrete quality.

It's a gift to listen. It costs nothing, but is of course, priceless.

Today's exercise is to truly listen to everyone you meet.

Say aloud to yourself, "I am worthy of good things."

Chapter Thirty-Three
Fire It Up

Fire is hypnotic and cleansing. One of my go-to brain-changing remedies is writing out my feelings and then releasing them by burning the paper.

Consider volcanos: These molten mountains literally create themselves from destruction. Drawing from a core deep within our earth, these global pressure points represent the exhalation of our planet. Whenever you purge your emotions via the written word and release them through fire, you are excavating your core.

Today's exercise (exorcise?) is to write about an issue in your life that is really bothering you. It could be a grudge; it could be simmering anger at a friend or family member. It could be a fear that has been lurking at the edges of your mind, perhaps related to an economic issue, or a relationship.

Set the timer and write for at least ten minutes – really pour out your guts onto the page. No one else is going to read this. Don't worry about spelling, syntax, or the legibility of your handwriting. None of those things matter. Your goal through this exercise is to just get it out of your head and onto paper.

Once you're done writing, go outside and burn it. Use a clay pot or another fire-safe receptacle, and set fire to your note. Writing and burning is a cathartic act. I find that I use this one a lot, especially if I have non-specific feelings of unease about any given situation.

The act of writing clarifies things for me, and watching my problem evaporate into wisps of smoke helps.

Say aloud to yourself, "I am worthy of good things."

Chapter Thirty-Four
Dorothy Parker Was Right

Flexing your curiosity muscle is a sure-fire way to change up your wiring and build resilience.

There is an intelligence that surrounds us of which we are largely ignorant. And not ignorant in the pejorative, meant-as-an-insult sense. Fact-based, as in not knowing or being literally unaware.

For example: Did you know that trees talk among themselves? Yep. Scientists are now discovering that plants have similar senses to ours and that they talk to each other — not through their roots, but as we do: through the air. It's amazing that there is so much that we do not yet know.

Have you ever read the book, Who Moved My Cheese? I use the premise of the four archetypes described within the book quite often when I consider the various sorts of folks who cross my path on a daily basis.

As an extremely abbreviated recap of the narrative, the concept of the book is that there exists a room with cheese. This cheese storage room gradually becomes empty, and there are four different types of mice who have varying responses to the cheese depletion status (Sniff, Scurry, Hem and Haw – representing four different types of people).

For example, as much as I love my mother, I know that she is squarely in the "Hem" camp. Of the four archetypes featured in the book, Hem is the most resistant to change. My mother, likewise, is the type of person who will continue to visit the empty cheese room, convinced that, surely, certainly, there will indeed be a new cheese shipment arriving any moment. Of course, alas, the cheese never arrives.

If you are reading this book, you are probably more like Sniff and Scurry, the two mice who adapt to and anticipate change. You may wish to be more independent, or are seeking to further your transition to a carefree, purpose-driven life, based on a resilient approach to situations. Curiosity is probably one of the best ways to get there, and I'm going to give you my $.02 as to why.

> Curious people try the path not taken.

> Curious people see if something will work.

> Curious people look under the hood.

> Curious people don't let things lie.

Want to boost your bravery levels? Curiosity is the impetus for bravery in some instances. The curious are driven, compelled even, by the need to know. As a result, the curious takes risks. They shove their fear into their figurative back pocket and explore the unknown.

If you are still reading, I know that I have found a kindred spirit. Curiosity is that feeling in your gut that almost goads you into action. It's what prompted you to buy this book. Your need to satisfy your curiosity is more powerful than your fear of failure. Good. That means that you are destined for great things, because the curious keep trying.

If you are curious, you are also probably an innovator. Which is a shiny way of saying "failure magnet." If you innovate, you are going to fail. That's how it works. So give yourself a pass for being a failure. Most people never get this far.

Most folks walking this planet are content to go about their daily business without looking too far afield. They stay in their lane; color inside the lines and keep their eyes fixed on the stuff right in front of them. They are living a life that they perceive to be safe, and that's perfectly oka-lee-dokalee. Your choices are your choices. You get to make yours; other people get to make theirs.

That said, curious people disembowel clocks. They rip apart business models. They disrupt stuff left and right. They probably spent a lot of time in the corner as kids. We curious folks can be maddening to people who would rather we just leave things alone. Status quo people get really frustrated with the curious.

However, you're in good company, as is evidenced by this excellent quote:

> "I keep six honest serving-men,
> They taught me all I knew;
> Their names are What and Why and When
> And How and Where and Who."
> – Rudyard Kipling

It is through this seeking that we develop expansion and resilience. The same curiosity that brought us Tang and the space program also brought us chocolate chip cookies, virtual reality, Futurama and the cure for polio. Seekers find.

New frontiers are peopled by the curious. As you seek, keep in mind: in order to glean the most from our experiences as we pursue information, it is important to dispassionately observe what we find.

Through trial and error, consistent (and mindful) questioning and a willingness to grow our awareness, we will find ourselves on a wonderful journey of growth and resilience, joining other seekers like author Dorothy Parker who said, "the cure for boredom is curiosity. There is no cure for curiosity." Thank goodness.

Today's assignment is to take something apart and then put it back together.

Say aloud to yourself, "I am worthy of good things."

Chapter Thirty-Five
Here There Be Dragons

The phrase "here there be dragons" is an aphorism that has come to define general fears of the unknown, based on an ancient cartographer's annotation to maps reflecting the earliest explorations of our globe. When mariners of epochs past would reach the end of their wanderings and the known world, they were have said to write "here there be dragons" (or lions in the case of the Romans) to represented uncharted territory.

What are your figurative dragons? For most of us, all of our dragons are manifestations of fear and doubt.

When you were a little kid, imaginary dragons and monsters lurked under the bed or in the closet. Show of hands: Who else besides me knew how to jump from the doorway to the bed at night so that the monsters couldn't grab your ankle and drag you under?

As you get older, adults know that the only things under the bed are fossilized Skittles, the renegade sock that escaped from the dryer and dust bunnies.

Our real fears live within the telephone we don't want to use when calling sales leads or funders.

They live in our gut when we have to ask for help.

They live in the mirror when we fear forgetting who we are.

What got rid of the monsters when you were a kid? For me, it was M&Ms, a flashlight and a mother who told me that I could vanquish the monster who lived at the dark end of the hallway on the way to my bedroom.

How do you banish monsters when you're an adult?

Surrounding yourself with good friends, the enlightenment within and of course, chocolate (if it ain't broke, don't fix it). I love fear now. Fear is my friend. When fear is present, I know that I am close to a breakthrough in my evolutionary journey of becoming a fully functional being.

The key to embracing fear is to understand what it represents. In order to do this, you'll need friends, paper, pencil and chocolate.

First of all, learn to recognize fear when it presents itself in your experience. How does it manifest for you?

    Is it irritability?

    Sweating?

    Dizziness?

    Sinking feeling in the gut?

Pay attention and when these twinges kick in, train yourself to ask, "What am I afraid of?" Journal about it in your notebook or otherwise record it.

Get to a place where you can process your answers, and your next step is to ask yourself, "Why am I afraid of this?" This step may take some time. Bring enough chocolate (by the way, the "why" is your flashlight).

Now, begin to explore the unknown. Through this exercise, you will prioritize and address your fears, and they will vanish like mirages in the desert. The paradox is (there's that word again), when fully faced and recognized for what they are, your fear (dragons/monsters) will evaporate.

To truly purge the power of your fear, have a good, long, healthy laugh at yourself for boxing at shadows. It is one of the most liberating feelings you'll ever experience.

What fears have you already overcome? How did you vanquish your dragons? Remind yourself of your successes when dealing with your fears. Resilience is fostered and developed by overcoming fear. Every little pinprick of doubt has its source in fear. Fears are like mold that fester in the dark parts of your soul. Faith and action are the light that banish such fungus and enable you to move forward.

For what's it's worth, in my opinion, fear is good. Fears are the hidden stumbling blocks that your subconscious sees (or perceives to be true). When those stabbing panic thoughts laced with fear surface, pay attention. Write them down. And then knock them down, one at a time.

You may listen to your fears, but do not heed them.

For extra credit: Flip the script: what happens if you fail?

Define failure. Losing your business? Losing your money or investment? Losing your family? Losing your life? Put some scope in the mix. There are those who think that oversimplifying things to this degree sounds childish, but in my opinion, it's not. Fear of imagined, yet unstated outcomes can be paralyzing. By transforming these imaginings out of your head and into the written word through journaling in your notebook, you can examine these paper tigers for what they really are.

Only when faced can your dragons be beaten. As a reminder, here's a great quote from author Neil Gaiman:

> "Fairy tales are more than true — not because they tell us dragons exist, but because they tell us dragons can be beaten." Earliest known attribution is an epigraph in Neil Gaiman, Coraline (2004)

Which is based on the full G.K. Chesterton quote:

> "Fairy tales, then, are not responsible for producing in children fear, or any of the shapes of fear; fairy tales do not give the child the idea of the evil or the ugly; that is in the child already, because it is in the world already. Fairy tales do not give the child his first idea of bogey.
>
> What fairy tales give the child is his first clear idea of the possible defeat of bogey. The baby has known the dragon intimately ever since he had

an imagination. What the fairy tale provides for him is a St. George to kill the dragon. Exactly what the fairy tale does is this: it accustoms him for a series of clear pictures to the idea that these limitless terrors had a limit, that these shapeless enemies have enemies in the knights of God, that there is something in the universe more mystical than darkness, and stronger than strong fear."

Today's exercise is to list three of your fears and identify their source. Naming your fears is the first step in relinquishing their power over you.

Say aloud to yourself, "I am worthy of good things."

Chapter Thirty-Six
How to Recognize Miracles

I blame Charlton Heston.

When I was a little kid, the yearly screening of The Ten Commandments was anticipated in our household for a number of reasons. The first of which was its role as a rite of passage to, if not adulthood, at least big kid status, proved through the ability to stay awake through the entire thing. Alas, for many years, my brothers and I would consistently conk out on the living room floor somewhere around Yul Brynner's "So let it be written; so let it be done" edict.

We yearned for the year when we could finally last until the second reason: the special effects, chief among them the parting of the Red Sea. Now this was a miracle!! Epic. Sweeping. Monumental. Supernatural and supernal. Seeing Chas up there on the rock, serving as the conduit for what God wrought below spoiled me for quite a while where miracles were concerned.

Would you recognize a miracle if you saw it?

Most of the time we want big and flashy, or at least it's what we expect from our miracles. The quiet ones like breathing, flowers blooming or a choice parking spot opening up for us on a rainy day? Meh.

Folks who follow me on twitter will note that I sign off most evenings with #poetry as my #goodnight tweet. One of my favorite poets is Walt Whitman, and his poem, Miracles is one of the reasons why. The poem lists a number of everyday events, observances and experiences, all of which exist within a confluence of everything: "The whole referring, yet each distinct and in its place."

As an example, for the women reading this, if (or when) you were pregnant, did it seem as though every other woman on the planet was pregnant? This perception grew from your awareness. You were attuned to pregnancy and everything that involves bearing a child; hence, you recognized this experience in those who surrounded you. It's the same with the awareness of miracles. The more miracles you acknowledge, the more of them that you will see.

Miracles are generated at the intersection of our internal and external worlds, through syncing the inner and outer environments. Through the symbiotic action of improving ourselves, we improve our environs by default. In so doing, we affect change and provide the catalyst for miracles.

Spoiler alert: Through the act of reading this book and following its precepts, you are enabling the formation of miracles.

For the sake of discussion, let's assume that miracles are evidence of the Divine. When we take active steps to nurture and develop our higher selves, are we not engaging the divine within? Taken a step farther, by engaging divinity, are we not giving it the opportunity to flex itself and to manifest itself in our lives?

You are the miracle.

You're a confluence of DNA, tRNA and other helix models twirling, replicating and creating worlds. The fact that you exist at all is, in and of itself, a miracle. Your thoughts, desires, mechanical dexterity and talents are all finely orchestrated cellular wonders. You are a carbon-based life form with sentience, a conscience and an ability to decide what your life is going to be. Every morning you have another 24 hours to make something happen.

Every morning is your birth day.

Today's exercise is to give thanks for every miracle you can recognize, from the mundane to the phenomenal.

Say aloud to yourself, "I am worthy of good things."

Chapter Thirty-Seven
More, Please

What if you've read this far and you're thinking, "Molly, you're sweet and all, but you are full of crap. You don't know anything about me or my situation, and some well-meaning suggestions won't do me any good. Thanks, but no. Keep your armchair quarterbacking for someone else."

Fair enough.

If you are in a space where what I've given isn't good enough, reach out to someone who can help. If you are experiencing persistent or clinical depression, you may require more than this book can provide. However, there are people on this planet who may be able to relate to what you are going through. There are over seven billion of us, so chances are good there is someone who will understand and can help you find the way.

It has been said that no lock is created without the key to unlock it. In the same fashion, there is no problem that you currently face that doesn't have it's solution within you. If you are in a scary, dark and lonely place where no help is immediately visible, reach out to these people. They will answer:

Call the National Suicide Prevention Lifeline at 1-800-273-8255 or visit www.suicidepreventionlifeline.org

YOU ARE WORTHY OF GOOD THINGS.

Ayuda en Español

Cuando usted llama al número 1-888-628-9454, su llamada se dirige al centro de ayuda de nuestra red disponible más cercano. Tenemos actualmente 150 centros en la red y usted hablará probablemente con uno situado en su zona. Cada centro funciona en forma independiente y tiene su propio personal calificado.

Veteran?

The Veterans Crisis Line connects Veterans in crisis and their loved ones with qualified, caring Department of Veterans Affairs responders 24 hours a day, 7 days a week, 365 days a year. For free, confidential support call 1-800-273-8255 and Press 1, chat online, or send a text message to 838255.

Author Biography

Molly Cantrell-Kraig is a speaker, media consultant and author, profiled by The Christian Science Monitor and listed among the CNN10: Visionary Women in honor of Women's History Month (March 2014), and featured as one of 32 global influencers in Social Media and Inspirational Leadership by the Huffington Post in February 2013.

As a speaker, Cantrell-Kraig covers topics as varied as building relationships between entrepreneurs and the media, women, poverty, social entrepreneurism, tech and impact investing. Cantrell-Kraig has appeared as either a speaker or panelist at NextGen:Charity in New York City; TechWeek Chicago and Pitch Week, Chicago. She was also invited to attend the premier episode of the Ricki Lake Show, in Los Angeles, where the episode featured online communities that had an impact offline. Additionally, Cantrell-Kraig has been profiled by WGN, The Shriver Report, the Women's Media Center in Washington, DC, Women's World Magazine, Bustle, and Autobody News. You may find Cantrell-Kraig on Instagram or Twitter as @mckra1g. She lives in Chicago, where you can find her near the lake or reading a book.

CPSIA information can be obtained
at www.ICGtesting.com
Printed in the USA
LVHW090120100819
627219LV00001B/48/P